D0463326

Camping

By Kristin Thoennes Keller

Consultant:
Johan Rindegard
Former Editor and Production Manager
Sierra Club Outings Department

CAPSTONE
HIGH-INTEREST
BOOKS

an imprint of Capstone Press
Mankato, Minnesota

Capstone High-Interest Books are published by Capstone Press
151 Good Counsel Drive, P.O. Box 669, Mankato, Minnesota 56002
http://www.capstone-press.com

Library of Congress Cataloging-in-Publication Data
Thoennes Keller, Kristin.
   Camping/by Kristin Thoennes Keller.
   p. cm.—(The great outdoors)
   Includes bibliographical references and index.
   ISBN 0-7368-0911-2
   1. Camping—Juvenile literature. [1. Camping.] I. Title. II. Series.
GV191.7 .T46 2002
796.54—dc21   00-012551

Summary: Describes the equipment, skills, safety issues, and environmental concerns
of camping.

Editorial Credits
Carrie Braulick, editor; Lois Wallentine, product planning editor; Timothy Halldin,
   cover designer and illustrator; Katy Kudela, photo researcher

Photo Credits
Capstone Press/Gary Sundermeyer, cover (bottom left, bottom right), 17, 23 (foreground),
   24, 26, 28, 31 (foreground), 36 (top, bottom), 37 (top)
Comstock, Inc., 1, 23 (background), 31 (background)
Fred Pflughoft/Gnass Photo Images, 20
Jeff Henry/Roche Jaune Pictures, Inc., 40
Joanne E. Lotter/TOM STACK & ASSOCIATES, cover (top right)
Jon Gnass/Gnass Photo Images, 4, 43
Kathy Adams Clark/KAC Productions, 38
Kent and Donna Dannen, 34
Photo Network/Margo Taussig Pinkerton, 7; Mark Newman, 9, 13, 14; Eric R. Berndt,
   10; G. R. Russell, 19; Chad Ehlers, 32
Visuals Unlimited/Mark E. Gibson, 37 (bottom)

1 2 3 4 5 6 07 06 05 04 03 02

Table of Contents

CHAPTER 1

Camping

Thousands of years ago, American Indians lived in many parts of North America. They often hunted animals such as buffalo for food. These Indians moved to follow the animal herds. They set up camps to sleep outside. They often camped for weeks or months at a time. Some American Indians never built permanent dwellings.

From 1848 to 1864, people camped during California's Gold Rush. Many North Americans traveled to California to look for gold during this time.

Today, most people camp for recreation. They may camp in a camper or a recreational vehicle. But the most popular type of camping is tent camping.

Campers sometimes set up tents in remote areas.

A Recreational Hobby

People camp for many reasons. Some campers enjoy observing a variety of plants and wildlife outdoors. Others enjoy the challenge of living outdoors. Some people camp to spend time with others.

Campers have many choices when they look for campsites. Many national parks and national forests provide campsites. State and local parks provide thousands of campsites to campers each year. Some of these campsites are established. These sites may have running water and bathrooms. They usually have fire rings. These areas can be formed from rocks placed in a circle. Other fire rings are round metal ridges. Campers can make campfires or use charcoal to cook in fire rings. Some campsites have raised steel grills for cooking.

Some campers prefer to camp in wilderness areas at non-established sites. These people may camp in mountains, forests, or deserts. Non-established sites do not have areas already prepared for camping.

Many people camp during spring and summer.

Planning the Trip

Responsible campers carefully plan their trips. They choose when and where they want to camp. Most people camp during warmer seasons. They learn about the camping area's normal weather conditions, landscape, and wildlife. They consider how crowded a certain campground normally is. Some people plan to fish, hike, or canoe during their camping trips.

These campers choose campgrounds that offer these activities.

Campers who plan to camp at established sites often need to make reservations. Many national and state park campgrounds fill up quickly. Campers make sure to make reservations well in advance of their trip. Campers sometimes need to obtain permits to enter public land or campgrounds.

Many popular campgrounds fill up quickly.

ALL PARK CAMPGROUNDS
ARE FULL

CHAPTER 2

Equipment

The amount of equipment campers bring varies with the type of trip. Campers who go to established sites at parks drive to the campgrounds. Other campers carry backpacks filled with supplies and walk to remote areas. But all campers need some basic items to keep them safe and comfortable.

Survival Gear

Campers need a compass and a map of the area. Many campgrounds provide maps. Campers who camp in wilderness areas may get a map from the land managers or owners.

Campers need firestarter, candles, a lighter, and waterproof matches. Campers can make a fire with these items to cook, keep warm, or signal others if they become lost.

Some campers bring recreational equipment such as bicycles and canoes.

Campers should pack these items in a waterproof container.

Other items are useful to campers. Campers can use a pocketknife to cut a bandage or untie a knot.

Campers should bring a first aid kit. These kits usually include items such as gauze, adhesive bandages, and ointment to protect wounds from germs.

Each camper should carry a whistle. A lost camper can blow the whistle. A whistle's sound carries farther than people's voices.

Campers also should carry a flashlight. They should make sure the flashlight's batteries are new.

A nylon rope is useful to campers. They can use the rope to tie food in a tree to keep it away from animals. A rope can hold together broken equipment. Campers also can use a rope to make a clothesline to dry clothing.

Campers should consider bringing money. They may need money to make a phone call or to buy food.

People who camp during winter should have warm, sturdy four-season tents.

Shelter

Campers usually bring a nylon tent for shelter. Most campers choose three-season tents. These tents keep campers warm in cool weather. Campers who only plan to camp during summer may choose two-season tents. These tents often have screens to allow air to move through them. Winter campers should choose four-season tents. These tents are warmer, sturdier, and heavier than other tents. They

Tents come in a variety of shapes.

have three or more poles. Other tents may have only two poles.

Campers can choose from tents of different shapes. For example, dome tents are round. A-frame tents are shaped like a triangle. The shape campers choose depends on their space needs. Campers who need a great deal of space often buy dome tents.

Campers should bring a plastic ground cloth to lay under the tent. A ground cloth helps keep the tent floor dry. It also can help campers stay dry during rain showers or thunderstorms.

Campers bring sleeping bags on their trips. These bags usually are made of down or synthetic fabrics. Down is made from feathers. Synthetic fabrics are made by people. These fabrics include polyester and nylon. Campers should choose sleeping bags that are warm enough for the area's weather.

Many campers place sleeping pads under their sleeping bags. The pads help hold in body heat. The most common sleeping pads are closed-cell foam mats and air mattresses. Closed-cell foam does not absorb moisture. This feature helps campers stay dry. Air mattresses are connected to an air pump. Campers turn a valve that controls the flow of air into the mattress.

Backpacks

Campers who use backpacks should make sure the packs are comfortable and strong. Most backpacks are made of nylon. The shoulder straps and back should be padded.

Backpacks should be large enough to carry all necessary camping equipment. Backpacks are measured in cubic inches. Most backpacks used for camping have at least 4,000 cubic inches (65,548 cubic centimeters) of space inside of them.

Clothing

Campers prepare for all types of weather. The weather often changes throughout the day. Most campers wear several layers of clothing. Layered clothing allows campers to add or remove clothing to maintain a comfortable body temperature.

The first layer of clothing should draw moisture away from the skin. Many campers choose synthetic fabric or wool for this layer. They may choose a synthetic fabric made from polyester called polypropylene. Campers should

Campers should dress in layers to remain comfortable.

not wear cotton next to their skin. Cotton does not dry quickly.

The middle layer of clothing should provide warmth and move moisture outward. Many campers wear a soft fabric called fleece for this layer.

The top layer of clothing should be a jacket. This jacket should be water-resistant and windproof. The jacket's fabric should be breathable or have slits to allow air to pass through it. This feature helps prevent campers from becoming too warm.

Experienced campers usually wear wool socks or socks made of synthetic blends. They do not wear cotton socks. Cotton often stays wet. The wet material can rub against campers' feet and cause blisters. These sore bubbles of skin are filled with liquid.

Campers need to wear comfortable shoes. Campers who plan to hike often wear hiking boots. These boots are sturdy and have soles with deep grooves. Some campers wear sneakers if they do not plan to hike a great deal.

Clothing to Pack

Campers usually pack lightly. They do not bring clean clothes for every day of their camping trip. They plan to wear clothes at least twice before they wash them.

Campers may pack one pair of shorts and one pair of pants for a trip lasting two to three nights. They may bring two short-sleeved shirts and one long-sleeved shirt or sweater. Campers usually

Campers plan their meals and bring all the necessary cooking supplies.

pack at least two pairs of socks in case the pair they are wearing becomes damp.

Food and Cooking Equipment

Campers bring food and cooking equipment. They plan their meals before they leave home. Many campers bring freeze-dried foods. These foods are dried to make them stay fresh for long periods of time. Many campers bring bacon, hamburger, and hot dogs. Other popular

Campers in wilderness areas sometimes purify water from natural sources to make the water safe to drink.

camping foods include chocolate bars, dried fruit, dried meats, canned soups, popcorn, and rice. Some campers pack instant meals, cereal, powdered milk, and cheese. Campers must make sure to keep fresh food such as meat in a cooler.

Campers often bring a small camping stove to cook their food. They bring fuel such as gasoline or propane for cooking. Campers also may build campfires. But some campgrounds have burning bans on campfires during periods of little rainfall. Fires can spread quickly during these times.

Campers at established sites usually have drinking and cooking water available. Other campers can bring equipment to purify water from natural sources. Water from streams, rivers, and lakes often contains germs that can make people sick. Campers can purify water with a water filter or use iodine tablets, crystals, or drops. They also can boil the water for three to five minutes to purify it.

Campers who use water from natural sources should bring at least 1 quart (.9 liter) of water from home. They may need the water if their campsite is far from natural water sources. They also may need to use the water for first aid.

Campers need to bring other cooking items. They should pack a cooking pot with a lid and handles. They may need to pack a can opener, pot holders, and aluminum foil. They should bring cups and silverware. Campers need a bowl for washing dishes, a dish cloth, and dish towels. Responsible campers bring biodegradable dishwashing liquid. This soap breaks down easily in the environment.

Other Items

Other items that campers bring depend on their personal needs. They may pack a bath towel, biodegradable body soap, and shampoo. They may bring a toothbrush and toothpaste. Some campers bring plastic trash bags of various sizes. Campers can use these bags to store trash, gear, and food. They also may line their backpack with trash bags to keep their gear dry.

Campers should pack items for outdoor protection. They need sunscreen and sunglasses to protect their skin and eyes from the sun. Campers may bring a hat with a wide brim to shade their face. Some campers bring insect and tick repellent. These lotions or sprays help protect campers from insect bites and ticks. Ticks attach themselves to skin to suck blood. Some ticks can cause diseases after they attach to the skin.

Equipment

- Tent
- Ground cloth
- Sleeping bag and pad
- Water and water purification equipment
- Food
- First aid kit
- Cooking, cleaning, and eating supplies
- Extra clothing
- Map
- Compass

- Flashlight
- Repair kit
- Insect repellent
- Sunscreen
- Firestarter, waterproof matches, lighter, candles
- Stove
- Rain gear
- Whistle
- Lantern
- Pocketknife
- Nylon rope

CHAPTER 3

Skills and Techniques

Campers often stop at an information center when they arrive at a campground. The workers can provide maps and answer campers' questions. They may tell campers about the weather forecast or the nearest medical center's location.

Choosing a Campsite

People who camp in campgrounds usually are assigned a campsite. Campers in the wilderness must choose their own site. This site should be as flat as possible. Campers should be careful not to damage the environment. They may choose to camp on gravel or sand instead of a place where many plants grow.

Campers may talk to park workers to learn about their camping area.

Campers set up their tents as soon as they arrive at their site.

Campers should avoid some places when they set up campsites. They should not camp near steep riverbanks or the edges of cliffs. Loose rocks could fall on campers in these areas. Campers should avoid setting up their site near hills. After rainfall, water may run down the hills and into these sites. Campers also should avoid areas where loose branches or dead trees could fall. Places with stones, sticks, or roots can make sleeping uncomfortable. Campers need to look for cleared ground.

Campers should set up their campsite at least 200 feet (61 meters) from a water source. This distance helps prevent soil erosion near the water source. Soil that wears away could run into the water. Campsites located away from water sources also prevent pollutants from entering the water.

Setting up the Tent

Campers usually set up their tent right after they arrive at their site. Many campers practice setting up their tent at home several times before their trip.

Campers follow several steps to set up their tent. They set aside the tent's poles, pegs, and stakes. They then stretch out the ground cloth and unroll the tent on top of it. Campers who have a freestanding tent place heavy objects on it. Campers with pegged tents stake the tent to the ground. Campers then insert the poles and pop up the tent. They should always check the stakes to make sure they are tight.

Many campers build campfires in fire rings.

Cooking

Campers must choose a place to cook.
They often use fire rings in established
campgrounds. Campers in wilderness areas
should make sure the campfire area is
sheltered from the wind. Campers should not
set up the cooking area directly below trees
with low branches. The branches could catch

fire. Campers also should try to choose a campfire site that has few plants.

Responsible campers follow safety guidelines before they cook. They make sure no burning bans are in effect. They avoid building fires in strong winds. They do not build a fire against large rocks. Fires can blacken rocks and cause them to crack. Campers should place a container of water nearby when they cook over campfires. They can use the water to put out stray sparks.

Campers should not use stoves in tents. Nylon can catch fire easily. A stove that is left on in a tent also can cause campers to become sick or suffocate. The fumes that stoves give off can make the air inside of the tent poisonous.

Meals

Campers can prepare a variety of meals over their campfire or stove. Pancakes and bacon or sausage are popular camp breakfasts. The noon meal usually is the simplest of the day. Many campers make sandwiches or heat soup at this time.

Campers usually eat their main meal in the evening. They often make hot dogs, hamburgers, chili, or steak. Campers may cook fish that they caught in a nearby stream or lake. Many campers make foil-wrapped meals. They wrap their food in aluminum foil and cook the package over hot coals.

Foil-Wrapped Meal

Ingredients:
1/4 pound ground beef, raw
1 diced medium potato
2 diced carrots
1/4 cup diced onion
Salt and pepper, as desired

Equipment:
Aluminum foil
Metal spatula
Fork

1. Place the ground beef in the center of a large piece of aluminum foil.

2. Cover the ground beef with the potato, carrots, onion, and salt and pepper. Fold the foil over all ingredients and seal securely at the top. Make sure the fold is tight. A tight package prevents the food juices from leaking.

3. Place the pack in hot coals.

4. Let the pack cook for 20 minutes. Turn the pack over and let it cook 25 minutes longer. Open the pack carefully and test for doneness. The meat should be brown. The vegetables should pierce easily with a fork.

Serves: 1   *Children should have adult supervision.*

Responsible Camping

Camping is a popular activity. Some campgrounds and wilderness areas are becoming overused. Plant life in these areas often is damaged. Soil in busy campgrounds sometimes erodes. Some campgrounds are polluted with litter.

Campers need to respect the environment. They should be careful not to trample plants or pollute water sources. They should deal with trash responsibly. Most established sites have trash cans. Wilderness campers put any trash they create into bags and carry it home with them. Campers who care about the environment also pick up trash left by other people.

Busy campgrounds are more likely to cause damage to the environment.

Campers who hike should stay on trails.

Shutting Down Camp

Responsible campers shut down their camp
properly before they sleep. They wash the
dishes. They hang food in a tree or pack it in
the trunk of a vehicle. These actions help
prevent animals from eating the food. Campers
also secure loose items at their campsite. These
items are less likely to be carried away by
the wind.

Campers also need to shut down their campfire areas properly. They should crush any large clumps of charcoal in fire rings. They should remove any trash or food from the ashes. Campers also should make sure no hot embers remain. These hot remains of the fire could restart it.

Hiking

Campers sometimes take hikes away from their campsite. Hikers should walk on trails. Hikers who do not follow trails may ruin plants or damage land.

Hikers should walk in single file to help keep the trail its original width. Hikers who wander off the trail can make the original trail wider or create another trail. Other people may then travel on the new trail and damage more land.

Building a Campfire

Gather wood for the fire near your campsite. Only use dead wood that is already on the ground. Gather small twigs to start the fire and large branches to add to the fire after it starts.

1. Make a pile of tinder. Use very small twigs. You also may add paper, dried leaves, moss, or dry grass to the twigs.

2. Build a teepee-shaped cone of branches around the tinder pile. Leave one side slightly open.

3. Add slightly larger branches around the cone's outside. Light the tinder through the opening. You may need to feed the fire with twigs or paper until the branches catch fire.

4. Continue to add wood after the fire is burning. Choose longer and thicker logs. Always maintain the shape of the teepee. Do not pile too many logs or branches on at once. This action can smother the fire.

Put out your campfire safely. Burn all the branches down. You may sprinkle water on the fire to make it burn out faster. Make sure no hot embers remain. Return any branches that you did not use to the place where you found them.

Leaves of three leave it be.
Leaves of five let it thrive.
Poison ivy, *Toxicodendron radicans*, (left)
has three leaflets which can
cause mild to severe skin irritation.

Virginia creeper, *Parthenocissus
quinquefolia*, (right) has five
leaflets and is commonly
mistaken for poison ivy.

CHAPTER 5

Safety

Responsible campers know how to stay safe. They handle campfires properly. They protect themselves from harmful plants. They stay safe during thunderstorms and cold weather conditions.

Safety around Animals

Safe campers are careful around animals. They should not approach animals. This behavior may threaten animals.

Many animals raise young during spring. Campers should be especially careful during this season. Animals may be more aggressive in spring to protect their young.

Campers put leftover food in bags and take it home with them. They do not scatter food on the ground. The food can harm animals that

Campers should be aware of harmful plants in the area.

Keeping Food Safe from Bears

Some people camp in areas where bears live. These areas are called "bear country." Bears are attracted to food and items with odors such as toothpaste, deodorant, and cooking clothes. Campers at established sites often pack their food and items with odors in the trunk of a vehicle to keep it safe from bears. Some parks provide bear-safe containers. People sometimes place their food and scented items in a nylon or cloth bag. They then tie the bag to a tree to keep it from bears. Some parks and campgrounds have ropes and lines in place for hanging bags. Other campers must find a tree to hang their bags. Campers should follow several steps to hang a bag in a tree:

1. Find a tree branch that is at least 25 feet (7.6 meters) above the ground.

2. Tie a stick or large rock to a rope that is at least 50 feet (15 meters) long.

3. Throw the rope's end that is attached to the rock or stick over the branch. The rope should be at least 4 feet (1.2 meters) from the tree's trunk. Pull hard on both ends to make sure that the branch will hold the bag.

4. Remove the rock or stick and tie the bag to the rope. The bag can be lined with a plastic bag to keep items inside dry.

5. Pull down on the free end of the rope to move the bag up. The bag should hang at least 8 to 10 feet (2.4 to 3 meters) above the ground.

6. Tie the other end of the rope tightly around the tree trunk.

7. Another food bag can be tied to the other end of the rope. Use a stick to move the bag up into the air. The bags should be equally weighted.

eat it. Animals also may learn to depend on human food near campgrounds. Some of these animals may lose their natural fear of people and become aggressive.

Safe campers learn if snakes live in their camping area. They find out if any of the snakes are venomous. These snakes produce poison. People that are bitten by venomous snakes can become sick or die. Campers need a snake bite kit in areas with venomous snakes.

Harmful Plants

Campers should learn to recognize and avoid harmful plants. Certain berries and mushrooms can cause illness or death if they are eaten.

Campers should stay away from poison ivy, poison oak, and poison sumac. These plants grow in many areas of North America. The plants release an oil that irritates the skin and causes it to itch. The oil may cause blisters and swelling.

Many campers wear pants and long-sleeved shirts to protect themselves from harmful plants. Campers should wash their hands and clothes immediately after their trip. The oil from poison ivy, oak, and sumac spreads easily.

Weather Safety

Campers sometimes must deal with rain showers and storms. Campers who are outside during storms should stay away from water sources, tall trees, and cliffs. Lightning is more likely to strike in these places. Campers sometimes find shelter under short trees in a forest during rain showers.

Experienced campers sometimes camp during winter or cold weather. These campers wear warm clothing such as heavy coats, hats, and mittens. The warm clothing helps prevent hypothermia. This condition occurs when a person's body temperature becomes too low. This low body temperature can cause confusion, exhaustion, and muscle stiffness. Hypothermia even may cause death.

Winter campers drink plenty of water and eat often to keep their energy high. In winter,

Winter campers should eat often to keep their energy level high.

campers need more energy than campers in other seasons to stay warm.

Safe campers pay attention to their surroundings. They are prepared for all weather conditions. These campers help make their camping trips more enjoyable.

Words to Know

biodegradable (bye-oh-dee-GRAY-duh-buhl)—a substance or object that breaks down naturally in the environment

compass (KUHM-puhss)—an instrument people use to find the direction in which they are traveling; a compass has a needle that points north.

embers (EM-burz)—the hot, glowing remains of a fire

erode (i-RODE)—to wear away; the soil of overused campgrounds may erode.

gauze (GAWZ)—a thin cloth used as a bandage

iodine (EYE-uh-dine)—a chemical element found in seaweed and salt water; campers use iodine to purify water from natural sources.

stake (STAYK)—a pointed post that can be driven into the ground

To Learn More

Ching, Jacqueline. *Camping: Have Fun, Be Smart.* Explore the Outdoors. New York: Rosen, 2000.

Hooks, Kristine. *Essential Camping for Teens.* Outdoor Life. New York: Children's Press, 2000.

Thoennes Keller, Kristin. *Hiking.* The Great Outdoors. Mankato, Minn: Capstone High-Interest Books, 2002.

Werner, Doug. *Backpacker's Start-Up: A Beginner's Guide to Hiking and Backpacking.* Start-up Sports. Chula Vista, Calif.: Tracks Publishing, 1999.

Useful Addresses

American Camping Association
5000 State Road 67 North
Martinsville, IN 46151

National Park Service Headquarters
1849 C Street NW
Washington, DC 20240

Parks Canada National Office
25 Eddy Street
Hull, QC K1A 0M5
Canada

Sierra Club
85 Second Street
Second Floor
San Francisco, CA 94105

Internet Sites

Go Camping America!—Kids Pages
http://www.gocampingamerica.com/kidspage

Leave No Trace Outdoor Ethics
http://www.lnt.org

The National Park Service
http://www.nps.gov

Parks Canada
http://www.parcscanada.gc.ca/parks/main_e.htm

Recreation.Gov
http://www.recreation.gov

Sierra Club
http://www.sierraclub.org

Index